THE ESSENTIAL GUIDE

WRITTEN BY
JULIA MARCH

CONTENTS

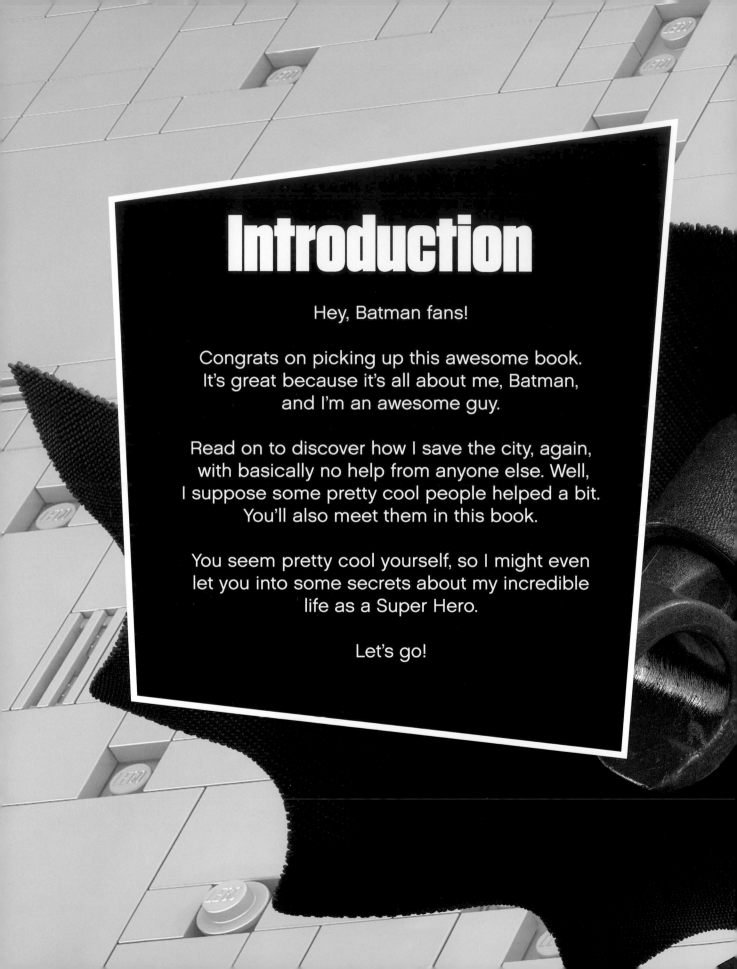

Introduction

Hey, Batman fans!

Congrats on picking up this awesome book.
It's great because it's all about me, Batman,
and I'm an awesome guy.

Read on to discover how I save the city, again,
with basically no help from anyone else. Well,
I suppose some pretty cool people helped a bit.
You'll also meet them in this book.

You seem pretty cool yourself, so I might even
let you into some secrets about my incredible
life as a Super Hero.

Let's go!

Batman

He is busy saving the city... again

Batman is awesome and he knows it. He is a Master Builder, a crime fighter and a hero to all who live in Gotham City. Despite his many fans, he is a proud solo Super Hero who says he does not need help from anyone. He never feels lonely, because he is too busy saving the city!

Batman's armoured face disguise is also called a cowl

ALWAYS BET ON BLACK!

Did you know?

Batman's butler, Alfred, thinks Batman's biggest fear is being part of a family again. Batman says his biggest fear is snake clowns.

Utility Belt holds all the gadgets Batman needs

Black is the new black

Batman has been around a long time, but his classic look means that he hasn't aged a day. His black suit helps him blend into the shadows and also makes the yellow of his bat-symbol really pop.

The Dark Knight
Like a real bat, Batman prefers to remain in the shadows and avoids daylight. Only at night does he take to the streets of Gotham City, ready to fight crime.

Best ways to contact Batman

Bat-Signal
Only switch this on if it is really important. The signal will shine brightly into the night sky.

Bat-phone
Batman might be busy. Enjoy the hold music or leave a message. He'll get back to you.

Bat Fax
It's slow and kind of old school, but you might just reach him.

Hand-held Batarang weapon in trademark black

Bright lights help Batman to spot criminals in the dark streets below

Bat shapes are part of Batman's iconic design style

Batman displays the bat-symbol front and centre on the Batwing

"Black Thunder"

Master Builder
There is nothing Batman can't create with his incredible building skills. He has a vehicle for every occasion, on land and in the air. He has named his latest Batwing model "Black Thunder."

Be like BATMAN

Batman is the coolest, toughest, most stylish and most awesome Super Hero ever. That is because he knows the most awesome thing is to be is yourself. He does have a few tips for fans who want to be like their hero though... because it's also cool to be like Batman.

Treat yourself

Super Heroes work hard to keep other people safe. As a reward for your hard work, why not treat yourself with your favourite meal? Batman eats caviar, fine steaks and lobster thermidor. He deserves it!

Phone!

AWESOME FACE!

Document everything

Selfies are a great way to record your heroic deeds. Take as many photos as you can and you will always have a reminder of your awesome adventures. You can also use them to decorate your home.

Have some alone time

A little "me time" can really help a hero to unwind. Find a space far from the hustle and bustle, and just chill. Batman relaxes by swimming lengths in the serene Wayne Manor pool... bliss!

Pursue your talents

Keep developing your talents and pursuing your dreams. As well as being a billionaire, Master Builder and crime fighter, Batman is a musical genius! He can sing, rap, breakdance and play the piano with one hand and one foot.

GET READY FOR MY SICK BEATS!

THE MOST SUCCESSFUL CITIZEN EVER

It's no surprise who tops the list of Gotham City's wealthiest citizens (again)... Bruce Wayne! Brave Bruce lost his parents at an early age, but has since risen to conquer the heights of the business world, He's officially the richest person in the city – and the most mysterious.

Bruce attends many glittering parties but rarely hosts one at his own home, Wayne Manor. What is he hiding? Bruce won't cave in and tell!

So what's next for the man who has it all? A new business venture for Wayne Enterprises? Marriage to one of Gotham City's high-society beauties? When asked, Bruce just smiles his dazzling smile. He isn't sharing his future plans. Maybe some dark night we'll find out!

Bruce's parents, Thomas and Martha Wayne, died shortly after this family photo was taken, leaving him an orphan.

"Call me **Bruce**, champ."

Bruce Wayne looks sophisticated at Police Commissioner Jim Gordon's recent retirement gala. He wore a white designer tuxedo, black bow tie and red carnation buttonhole.

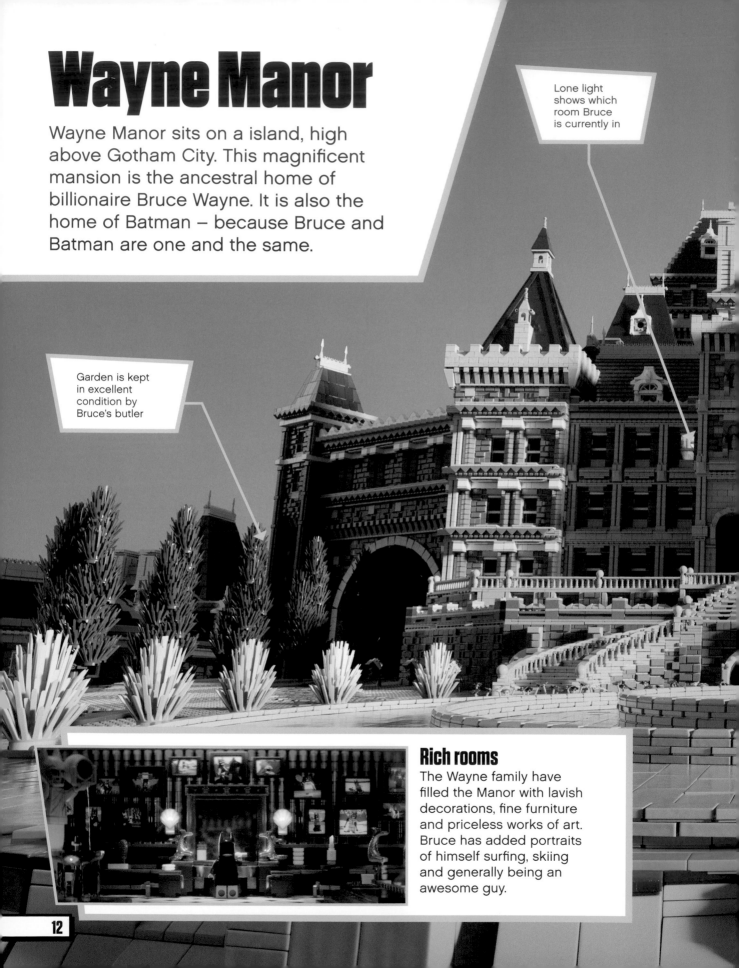

Wayne Manor

Wayne Manor sits on a island, high above Gotham City. This magnificent mansion is the ancestral home of billionaire Bruce Wayne. It is also the home of Batman – because Bruce and Batman are one and the same.

Lone light shows which room Bruce is currently in

Garden is kept in excellent condition by Bruce's butler

Rich rooms

The Wayne family have filled the Manor with lavish decorations, fine furniture and priceless works of art. Bruce has added portraits of himself surfing, skiing and generally being an awesome guy.

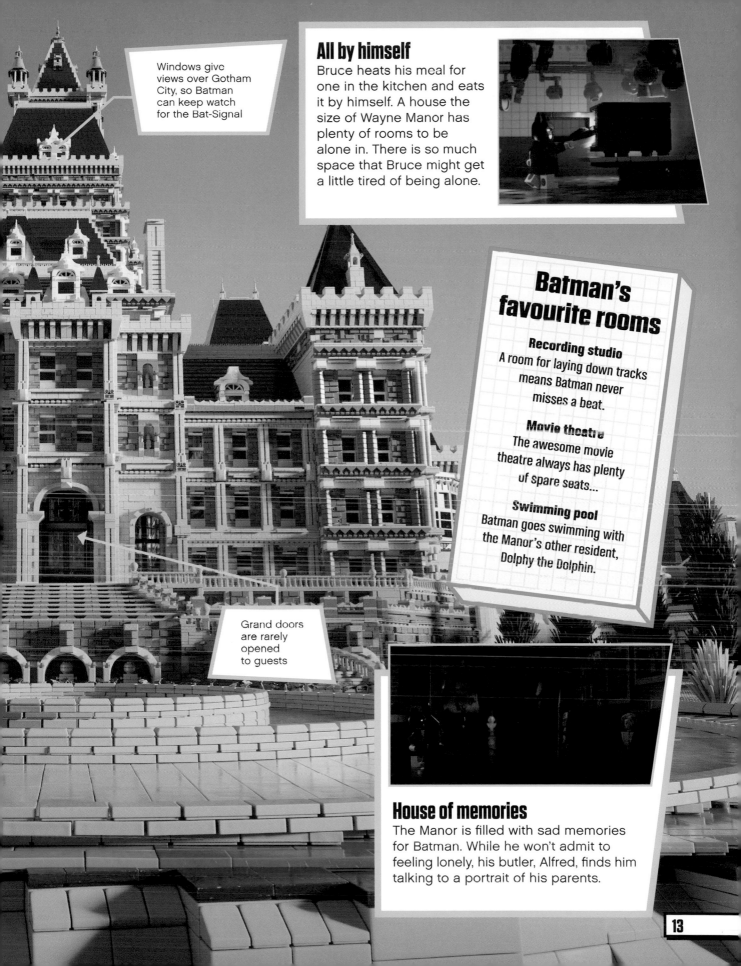

Windows give views over Gotham City, so Batman can keep watch for the Bat-Signal

All by himself

Bruce heats his meal for one in the kitchen and eats it by himself. A house the size of Wayne Manor has plenty of rooms to be alone in. There is so much space that Bruce might get a little tired of being alone.

Batman's favourite rooms

Recording studio
A room for laying down tracks means Batman never misses a beat.

Movie theatre
The awesome movie theatre always has plenty of spare seats...

Swimming pool
Batman goes swimming with the Manor's other resident, Dolphy the Dolphin.

Grand doors are rarely opened to guests

House of memories

The Manor is filled with sad memories for Batman. While he won't admit to feeling lonely, his butler, Alfred, finds him talking to a portrait of his parents.

Alfred Pennyworth
Butler in the Batcave

Alfred is Batman's butler. He is also the closest thing to family the Dark Knight has, having raised him since Bruce was a child. As well as keeping Wayne Manor running like clockwork, Alfred is a wise advisor who understands Batman better than Batman understands himself.

> AT YOUR SERVICE, MR WAYNE!

White collar is always starched to perfection

Traditional butler's coat with tails

Dedicated and dapper

Alfred's duties go far beyond those of most butlers, but he insists on wearing traditional butler's attire. He wears a striped waistcoat, a blue tailcoat, grey trousers and a crisp white collar.

Battling butler

Long ago, Alfred served in the British Royal Air Force. His military experience gives him the skills to help Batman with mechanics and technology in the Batcave.

Did you know?

Although he is Batman's employee, Alfred has a lot of power. He can deactivate the Batcomputer and even ground Batman if he wants to.

Wise words

Alfred knows Batman is secretly lonely. He believes Batman would be happier if he opened his home and heart to more people.

Alfred's daily chores

Preparing dinner
Alfred cooks a mean lobster thermidor – Batman's favourite dish.

Grouting bathroom tiles
After reaching the second bathroom of the fifth bedroom on the 17th floor, he's getting good at it.

Guarding the Manor
Not much gets past Alfred!

The Batcave

Deep below Wayne Manor lies the Batcave, the Dark Knight's secret headquarters. It contains a computer, costumes, vehicles, weapons and gadgets, all built by and for Batman. *Just* Batman! Nobody would dare touch his Batcave things. Not that they could, because only Batman and Alfred know about the Batcave... until now.

Batcomputer

Batman relies on the Batcomputer to gather vital information. He is annoyed when Alfred puts a parental lock on it to make Batman focus on parenting his new adopted son, Dick Grayson.

Automated walkways help Batman move around the vast space

Batman's wardrobe

This huge, mechanised closet contains a look for every occasion. Outfits, from Batsuits to bathrobes, hang on moving rails. Batman simply grabs the one he wants as it glides by.

Outfit options hang from mechanical hangers

Cell for any villains who dare to enter the Batcave

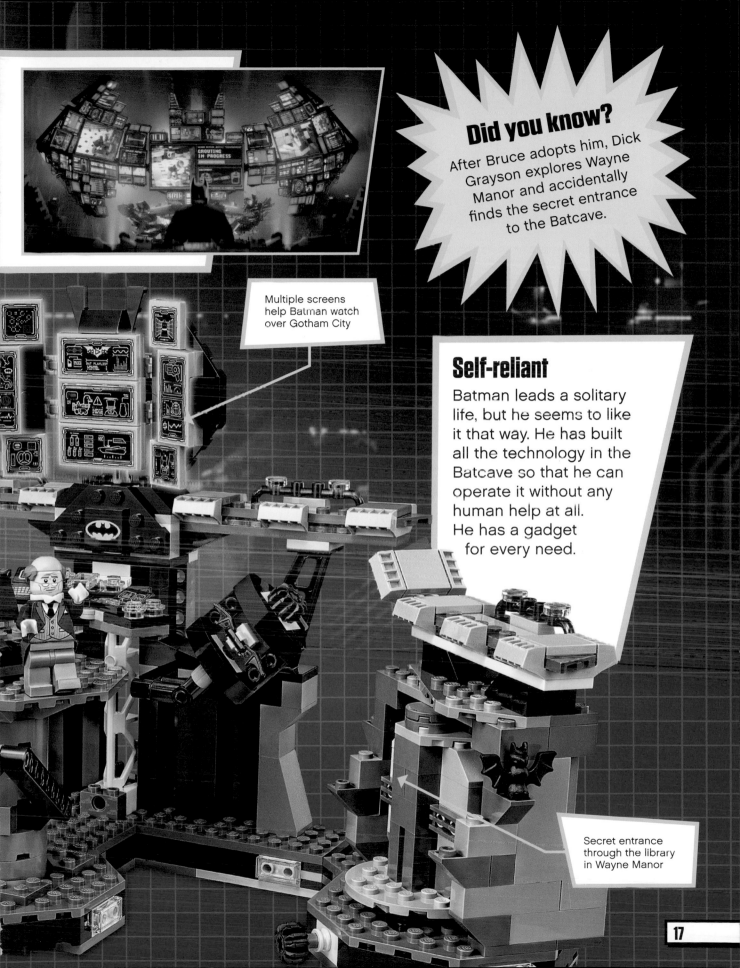

Did you know?

After Bruce adopts him, Dick Grayson explores Wayne Manor and accidentally finds the secret entrance to the Batcave.

Multiple screens help Batman watch over Gotham City

Self-reliant

Batman leads a solitary life, but he seems to like it that way. He has built all the technology in the Batcave so that he can operate it without any human help at all. He has a gadget for every need.

Secret entrance through the library in Wayne Manor

Build it like BATMAN

Batman loves vehicles. Cars, spaceships, zeppelins, kayaks, he's built them all – often right in the middle of a battle! He's quick with a brick and great with a plate, and that's how he earned the title of Master Builder.

Batman's garage

Batman is proud of the vehicles that fill the Batcave's garage. He built them all himself (with a little help from Alfred). He won't let anyone else touch them – fingerprints on a Bat-vehicle are a no-no!

Red fins are built into the rear of the craft

Low-level cockpit protected by clear windscreen

Batboat

The Dark Knight is a real warrior of the waves. Water-based enemies get a sinking feeling when they see the Batboat's two missiles and four blasters pointed in their direction.

"Riptide"

A secret trigger launches powerful missiles at foes

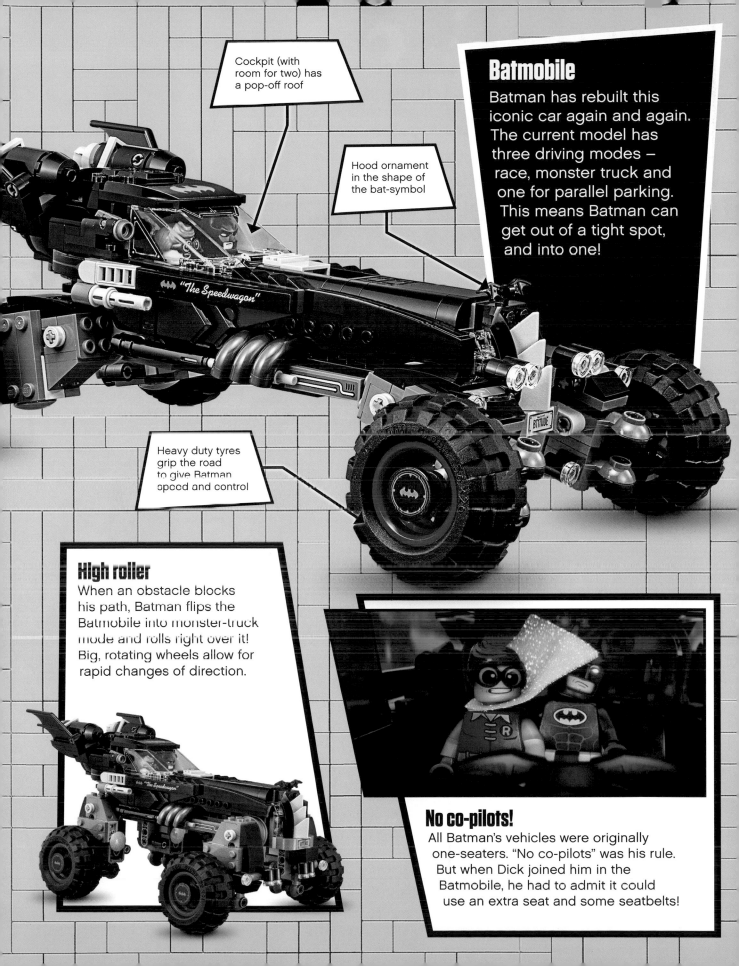

Cockpit (with room for two) has a pop-off roof

Hood ornament in the shape of the bat-symbol

Batmobile

Batman has rebuilt this iconic car again and again. The current model has three driving modes – race, monster truck and one for parallel parking. This means Batman can get out of a tight spot, and into one!

Heavy duty tyres grip the road to give Batman speed and control

High roller

When an obstacle blocks his path, Batman flips the Batmobile into monster-truck mode and rolls right over it! Big, rotating wheels allow for rapid changes of direction.

No co-pilots!

All Batman's vehicles were originally one-seaters. "No co-pilots" was his rule. But when Dick joined him in the Batmobile, he had to admit it could use an extra seat and some seatbelts!

I LOOK PHENOMENAL!

Tuxedo party
Batman has a jazzy range of tuxedo suits. He has a tuxedo dress-up party when he just can't decide which one to wear.

Raging Batsuit
Batman has punch lines for all the Joker's jokes when he laces on his purple boxing gloves. Pow!

Batman's wardrobe

Whatever Batman's doing, he has an outfit for every mission. His iconic black Batsuit is the most famous, but there are many more that he wears for training, action or just chilling out. Here is a small selection from his bat closet… all washed, pressed and waiting for the Dark Knight to slip into.

Vacation Batman
Batman makes sure his holiday goes swimmingly with his wetsuit, flippers and duck inflatable ring.

Caveman Batman
Even a sophisticated Super Hero like Batman sometimes likes to unleash the caveman within!

Scu-Batsuit
There's no time to take a breather on underwater missions. Luckily, this scuba suit is equipped with an oxygen mask.

Glam Rocker Batman
Batman is a heavy-metal, rapping machine, as this flamboyant silver suit with spiked epaulettes shows.

Bat-Pack Batsuit
Batman likes to express the showman side of his personality in this gold, Las Vegas-style suit.

Fairy Batmother
Batman's wish for Gotham City's villains to disappear might just come true with a wave of his magic wand.

Relaxed Batman
Alone in Wayne Manor, Batman slips into something comfortable, yet still stylish – a dark red silk robe.

The Joker

He will laugh until you cry

Did you hear the one about the green-haired villain with the evil smile? He is the Joker, and he claims to be Batman's worst foe – his nemesis. The Joker uses comedy weapons and is quick with a quip, but his latest plan to take over Gotham City is far from funny.

The Joker card shows he is ready to deal out destruction

FACE IT BATMAN, WE NEED EACH OTHER!

Did you know?

The Joker steals a plane that is being flown by best friends, Captain Bill and Captain Dave. They were not expecting to be joined by a new co-pilot named Captain Joker!

Pockets on waistcost to hold more joke items

Funny colors

Purple and green should *always* be seen according to the Joker (maybe with some yellow for contrast). He is very serious about looking dapper as he goes about his criminal funny business.

Three-step Joker plan

1. Steal the weapons onboard a cargo plane
Buckle up! Safety is no laughing matter on Joker Airlines.

2. Break into the Energy Facility
Cut out Gotham City's power. There will be no internet!

3. Take control of Gotham City
Banish Batman and impose hilarious rules. Ha ha!

A whole lot of history

After years of fighting, the Joker feels that he and Batman have a special relationship. Batman scoffs at the idea, wiping the smile right off the Joker's face.

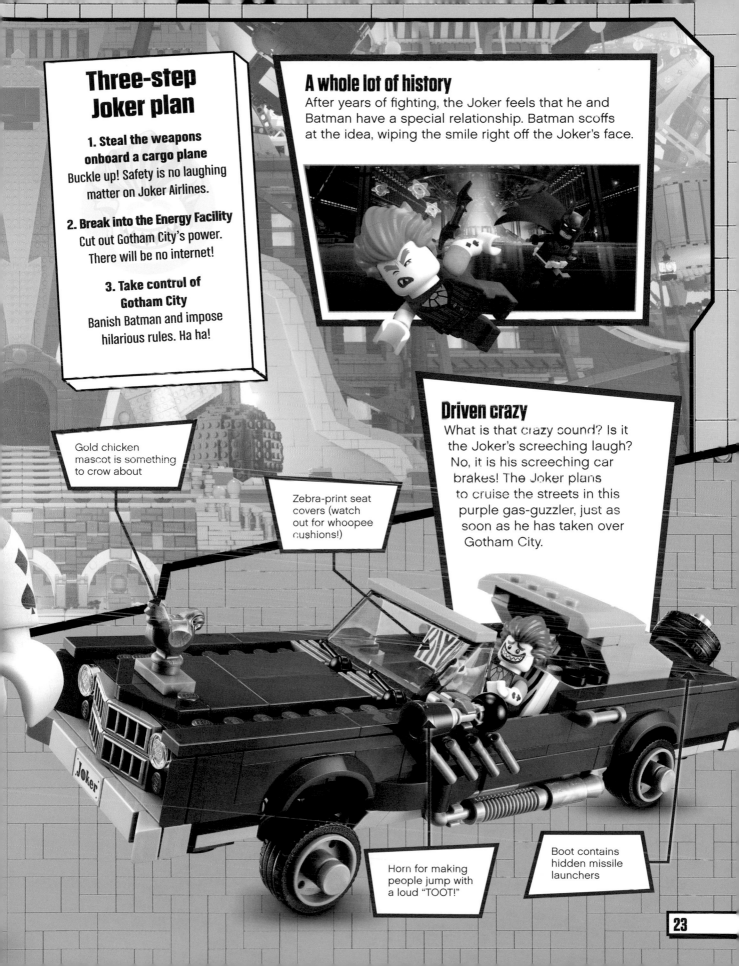

Driven crazy

What is that crazy sound? Is it the Joker's screeching laugh? No, it is his screeching car brakes! The Joker plans to cruise the streets in this purple gas-guzzler, just as soon as he has taken over Gotham City.

Gold chicken mascot is something to crow about

Zebra-print seat covers (watch out for whoopee cushions!)

Horn for making people jump with a loud "TOOT!"

Boot contains hidden missile launchers

Rogues Gallery

The Joker has assembled a group of the baddest baddies in all of Gotham City to help him with his latest scheme. These repeat offenders have taken more swipes at Batman than you can shake a brick at. Their criminal talents have won them a special place in the Joker's team... and in Batman's Rogues Gallery.

Guess who...

Which villain likes to baffle Batman by leaving hard-to-solve clues to his crimes? It's the Riddler, of course... no question about that!

Villain name The Riddler
Real name Edward Nygma
Powers Cunning mind

· The Riddler ·

Cold-hearted criminal

Mr Freeze thinks Batman should chill out, and he's ready with his freeze gun to make our hero do just that. Don't take his cryo suit away, though, or he'll really lose his cool.

Villain name Mr Freeze
Real name Dr Victor Fries
Powers Great strength and the ability to turn anything into ice with his freeze gun

Mr Freeze

Swooper villain

There's more than one bat in Gotham City – meet Man-Bat! Crime rates have hit record highs since this fly guy took to the skies.

Villain name Man-Bat
Real name Dr Kirk Langstrom
Powers Flight and razor-sharp claws

Man-Bat

Big bad guy

Bane is his name and pain is his game. This masked criminal has beefy muscles and a big beef with Batman. The Dark Knight better watch out for Bane's fearsome fists!

Villain name Bane
Real name Bane
Powers Super-strength

Bane

Poison Ivy

Eco-warrior

Keep away from Poison Ivy! She'll wrap you in her tendrils and trap you with her toxins. Batman just can't weed out this plant-loving foe – her criminal roots are too deep!

Villain name Poison Ivy
Real name Pamela Lillian Isley
Powers Able to control plant life

Catwoman

Wild wrestler

Killer Croc may be slow of brain, but when it comes to action he's pretty snappy. He's scaled up his attack ability with a monster truck that is as tough as his thick skin.

Villain name Killer Croc
Real name Waylon Jones
Powers Incredibly strong and really fast

Killer Croc

Beyond the claw

Meow! Catwoman has clawed her way to the top of Gotham City's criminal elite. She's a swift and stealthy cat burglar who usually gets away with it... by a whisker!

Villain name Catwoman
Real name Selina Kyle
Powers Nimble and crafty

Heads or tails?

Two-Face makes his decisions by flipping a coin. What will he be today? A friend and ally of Batman? Or a vile villain who wants to flip Batman head over tail into oblivion?

Villain name Two-Face
Real name Harvey Dent
Powers Extremely clever

Two-Face

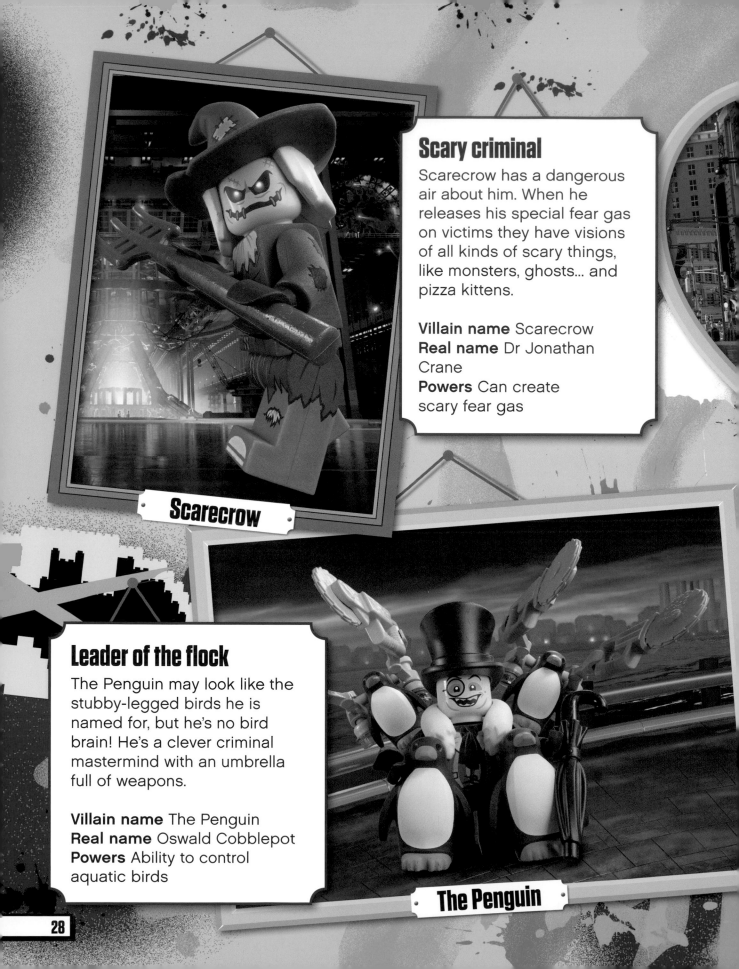

Scary criminal

Scarecrow has a dangerous air about him. When he releases his special fear gas on victims they have visions of all kinds of scary things, like monsters, ghosts... and pizza kittens.

Villain name Scarecrow
Real name Dr Jonathan Crane
Powers Can create scary fear gas

Scarecrow

Leader of the flock

The Penguin may look like the stubby-legged birds he is named for, but he's no bird brain! He's a clever criminal mastermind with an umbrella full of weapons.

Villain name The Penguin
Real name Oswald Cobblepot
Powers Ability to control aquatic birds

The Penguin

Quinn of hearts

Harley Quinn is a former doctor who now thinks laughter is the best medicine. She believes the Joker is one funny guy and he relies on his girl buddy to help out with all his criminal activities.

Villain name Harley Quinn
Real name Dr Harleen Frances Quinzel
Powers Highly intelligent and very agile

Harley Quinn

Messy mud man

Clayface is made of clay, so he's guaranteed to stick around in any battle. He fights dirty, too. Really dirty. In fact, he has been known to throw dirt in Batman's eyes!

Villain name Clayface
Real name Basil Karlo
Powers Mouldable body

Clayface

Rogue riders

Each of the Rogues has their own ride, and the Joker has gathered them all together for an attack on the Gotham City Energy Facility. From Killer Croc's chunky truck to the Riddler's sleek racer, each vehicle is full of nasty surprises that will help the Rogues to crash the power plant.

Crime boss
The Joker rallies the Rogues together from afar. He quickly organises them into attack formation!

Two-Face has transformed half of his truck into a wrecking machine

Catwoman is used to making a quick getaway on her Catcycle

Harley's cannon truck is equipped with speakers – making it as loud as she is

WHAT RHYMES WITH TEDDY?

PREPARE FOR A SCARE!

Propellers help keep the Scarecopter in the air

Killer Croc steers his truck from the rear, as he is too big for the cab!

Menacing motors

Each of these vile vehicles has been built for battle. Two-Face's tough truck is perfect for knocking through barriers, while the Catcycle is easy to manoeuvre into tight spots. Up in the sky, Scarecrow can drop fear gas from his Scarecopter.

Six wheels are better than four, as far as Bane is concerned

The Riddler knows that the lights on his car are a bright idea

JUST SAY YOU'RE READY, RIDDLER.

It's got to be one or the other, Batman. Save the city or catch your greatest enemy.

Who else do you have an intense super-cool relationship with?

Are you seriously saying that there is nothing – NOTHING – special about us?

Worst enemies

Batman and the Joker are never surprised to find themselves fighting. These two foes have been battling for so long the Joker thinks they have a special connection. Batman does not believe that they have a special relationship at all.

You think you're my greatest enemy?

I don't currently have a bad guy.
I am fighting a few different people.

There is no "us". Never has
been, never will be. You're
a clown who means
nothing to me.

Jealous Joker vs Bored Batman
The Joker loves his regular fights with
Batman. It upsets him when Batman
says has so many enemies, he can't
pick just one worst foe. After all, Batman
says he does not need anyone special in
his life, not even a worst enemy. The
Joker will have to do something more
extreme to get Batman's attention!

Barbara Gordon

Gotham City's new Police Commissioner

There's a new Police Commissioner in Gotham City. Barbara Gordon takes crime seriously, but she can't get Batman to take her seriously. Barbara knows she and the Dark Knight must work together – but he insists he doesn't need her help.

> TEAMWORK MAKES THE DREAM WORK!

Babs' Resume

Academic achievements
Top of her class at Harvard for Police.

Practical experience
Responsible for cleaning up crime in a neighbouring city.

Special skills
Inspirational speaker and motivator.

Megaphone to rally teammates and communicate with villains

Gotham City Police Department badge

Dressed to arrest

Barbara is a no-nonsense cop, and likes no-nonsense clothes. From her leather gun holster to her black trousers, all her clothes are practical and comfortable.

Did you know?

Barbara has many skills, as well as her policing abilities. She is a highly trained pilot, able to fly many types of aircraft.

Pink?! No thanks!

It takes several shots from Batman's Merch Gun to produce the perfect Super Hero outfit for Barbara. This pink option was not Barbara's style at all!

Vibrant purple cowl

Handcuffs for restraining captured villains

Yellow Utility Belt for gadgets

Change of clothes

Batman finally agrees to work with Barbara – and convinces her she needs a Super Hero identity, too. Batgirl's suit has all the features and gadgets that she needs to be at the top of her crime-fighting game.

Buckled boots give a firm grip

Batgirl
Gotham City's new Super Hero

Barbara's plan

Old Police Commissioner Jim Gordon used to call for Batman at the first sign of trouble. The new Police Commissioner, Jim's daughter Barbara, wants the Gotham City Police Department (GCPD) and Batman to team up instead. Her inspiring speech gets nearly all the citizens of Gotham City behind her plan. Only Bruce Wayne is not so sure it is a good idea.

- We're going to change the way we do things around here.

- It takes a village... not a Batman.

- My dream is for the police force to team up with Batman!

- Together, we could clean up these crime-ridden streets... forever!

Retirement gala

Commissioner Jim Gordon's retirement gala was the city's biggest event of the year. Gotham City's elite all turned out to say thank you to Jim and wish him well on his safari holiday. They also met the new Police Commissioner, Barbara Gordon.

The rich and famous citizens of Gotham City gathered to celebrate the careers of two top cops – Jim Gordon and his daughter, Barbara.

The sweet sound of angelic voices filled the air. OK, the choir weren't really angels... they were orphans. But they sure sounded heavenly.

The night's most heartwarming news was that Bruce Wayne has adopted one of the orphans from the choir. Well, that's the rumour!

The organisers made the venue look dazzling. Towering ice sculptures twinkled and gleamed around the venue, City Hall.

Billonaire Bruce Wayne arrived in a great-fitting tuxedo. He gave reporters not one, not two, but three red carpet poses. Looking good, Bruce!

New Commissioner Barbara has a great idea to try and combat crime. Her plan is to persuade Batman to team up with the police.

The gala was going with a swing until the Joker crashed the party. Fortunately, Batman was soon on the scene to deal with the uninvited guest.

Master Builder Checklist

Stud shooters

 Twin stud shooters on the cockpit and arms enable Batman to really hit the villains where it hurts.

Net firing

 A rotating shooter fires a net at villains, trapping them, and making a mess of their plans.

Extendable arm

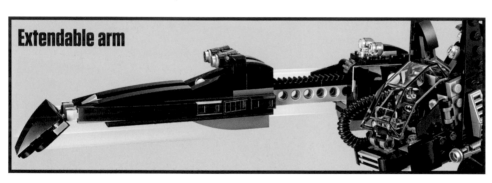

 By extending the Scuttler's arms, Batman gains a massive height advantage. Heads up, villains!

Bat pack

 Batman clips on the secret inbuilt jetpack to engage in aerial fights with his foes.

INITIALISE MASTER BUILD MUSIC!

The Scuttler

When the Joker and his gang crash Jim Gordon's retirement party, Batman needs to build something that can take out multiple targets with minimal damage. The Batcomputer has just one suggestion – the Scuttler.

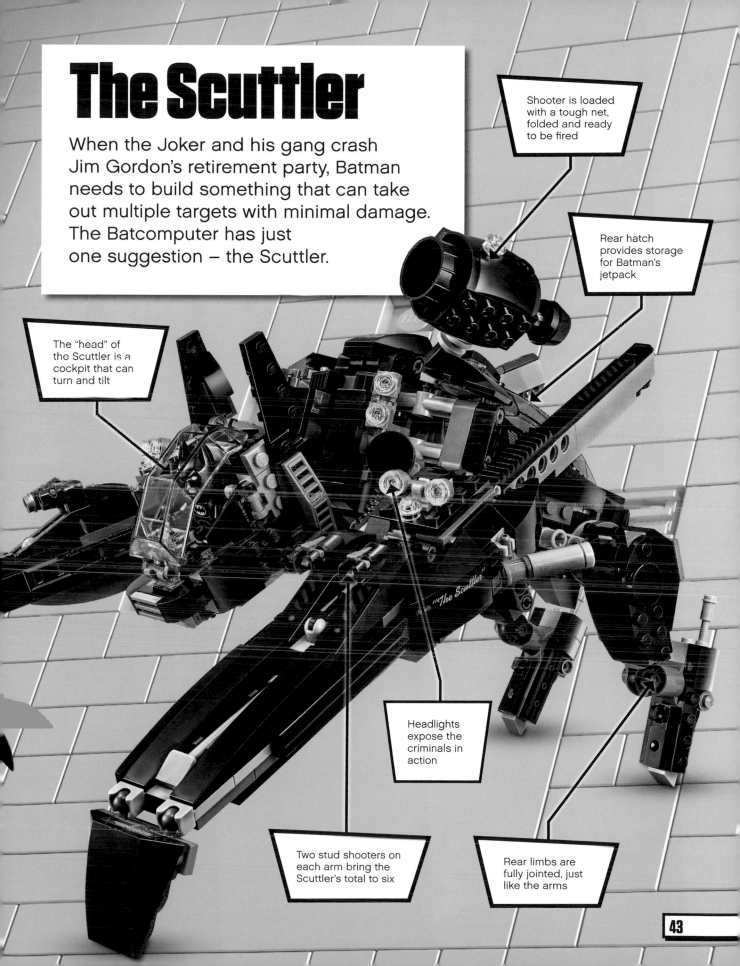

Shooter is loaded with a tough net, folded and ready to be fired

Rear hatch provides storage for Batman's jetpack

The "head" of the Scuttler is a cockpit that can turn and tilt

Headlights expose the criminals in action

Two stud shooters on each arm bring the Scuttler's total to six

Rear limbs are fully jointed, just like the arms

Arkham Asylum

Arkham Asylum! Just the name can make criminals cower. The gates of this grim, cold, dark prison have clanged shut on all Gotham City's bad guys, but the Rogues are true regulars. They even have their own high-security wing in the basement!

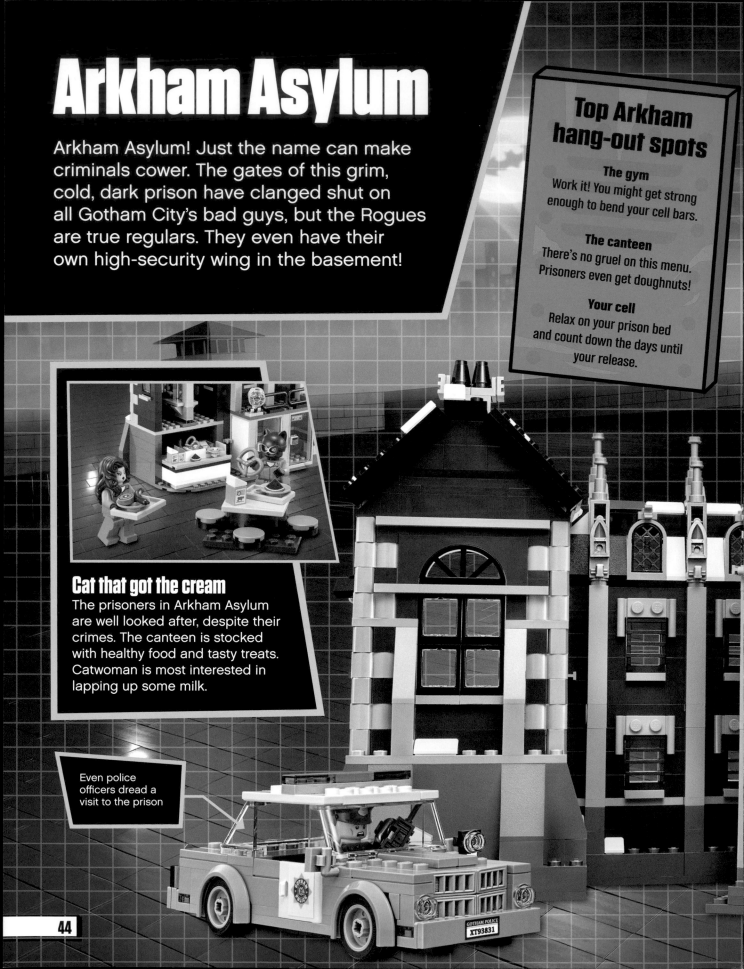

Cat that got the cream

The prisoners in Arkham Asylum are well looked after, despite their crimes. The canteen is stocked with healthy food and tasty treats. Catwoman is most interested in lapping up some milk.

Even police officers dread a visit to the prison

Ornate details are traditional in Gotham City architecture

Zoning out

The Joker is a regular at Arkham Asylum, but he does not want to go back! He plots to trick Batman into sending him to a different prison called the Phantom Zone. It is another of his plans!

Watchtower allows the guards to survey the whole prison site

ARKHAM ASYLUM

Foliage creeps through the barred windows of Poison Ivy's cell

Top 10

weirdest villains in Gotham City

Some of the villains in Gotham City are weirder than others. The Joker looks practically ordinary next to some of the extraordinary criminals on the streets. Batman is always busy keeping this strange bunch under control.

2

March Harriet

This costumed crook keeps her identity secret with an outlandish outfit. Not afraid to stand out from the crowd, March Harriet often works with a gang of fantastical criminal characters.

4

The Calculator

According to this villain's calculations, crime really does pay. The Calculator is a genius inventor who has created a computer that can predict the outcomes of battles.

1

Calendar Man

Calendar Man never misses an appointment with crime, thanks to his obsession with dates and holidays. He should watch out, or he will be counting down the days of a lengthy prison spell.

3

Kite Man

Look out! Kite Man is equipped with a glider and kite weapons so he can attack from the skies. Gotham City needs a strong breeze to blow this baddie away.

8

The Eraser

A friend to every villain in the city, the Eraser is an expert in cleaning up crime scenes. After he has erased the evidence, even Batman will struggle to crack the case.

6

The Mime

Ssshhh! The Mime enjoys a bit of peace and quiet, even as she commits her crimes. Her silent stealth and noiseless martial arts skills make it hard to hear her coming.

Orca

This marine biologist mixed her DNA with a killer whale and was transformed into Orca. She is making waves in the criminal underworld thanks to her excellent swimming ability.

10

Kabuki Twins

The Kabuki Twins cause double trouble for Batman and the rest of Gotham City. This pair of acrobatic bodyguards each have razor-sharp blades on both hands.

5

Red Hood

Nobody knows who hides under Red Hood's red hood. All the GCPD know is that they would like to lock him up in Arkham Asylum for all of his crimes. They will have to catch him red-handed first: though!

7

King Tut

King Tut is a royal pain in Batman's side. This deluded criminal thinks that he is a Pharoah and should rule over Gotham City. He is willing to cause chaos to bring his subjects under his control.

9

MY HERO IS...

I can't believe it. A month ago I had no dad, then I had one dad, now I have two dads! And get this... they're the exact two dads I'd have chosen out of all the dads in the world. They're my top two all-time heroes – Bruce Wayne and Batman. Best dads EVER!

Bruce Dad

Dad is the most successful orphan ever, and the nicest. He was so happy to adopt me – all I had to do was ask. I expect I remind him of himself when he was a kid!

Wayne Manor is my new home. It is VERY grand.

Good ideas for finding a dad*

- Sing in a choir

- Attend gala events

- Teeth whitener

- Practise making eyes larger and more vulnerable looking

* Luckily Dad likes me just the way I am.

MY DADS

by Dick Grayson

Batman Dad

I told Batman it was awesome that he lived in Bruce Wayne's basement, but he said I'd got it wrong. It's Bruce who lives in Batman's attic!

Batman says photos are banned in the Batcave, but I got this one.

Helping Batman

Batman didn't want me to come on missions at first. He must have been worried about my safety. I didn't let him stop me finding an awesome costume though!

LET'S GET GROOVING!

Those trousers were slowing me down!

Mission plan

Batman asks the Batcomputer for tips on sending the Joker to the Phantom Zone. The Computer reveals that Batman will need to get hold of the Phantom Zone Projector. But that won't be easy. It's in the hands of Batmans' archrival – Superman!

CHANCE OF FAILURE: 110%

Get the projector

The Phantom Zone Projector transports villains to the Phantom Zone, which is a prison in another dimension. Superman sends his worst enemies there. The projector is stored inside an atomic cauldron in Superman's Fortress of Solitude.

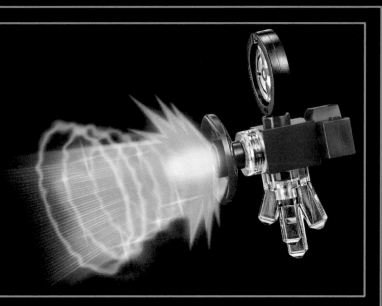

Avoid the laser grid

A laser grid guards the atomic cauldron. This is a two-hero job. Someone must wait above the grid ready to enter the cauldron, while someone else destroys the knowledge crystal that controls it. Get it right first time, or get zapped.

Potential hazards

Ring of napalm
Watch out for a boom from this explosive trap.

Acid moat
Your plans will dissolve if you fall in here.

Jaws of death
Only snappy movers can dodge this trap.

GOOD IDEAS BATMAN HAS HAD:

5, 678, 483

GOOD IDEAS EVERYONE ELSE HAS HAD: 0

110% RISK FACTOR

Batman will not be able to enter the atomic cauldron. His buff shoulders are too big for its 2.13 cm entrance. This job needs somebody small, super nimble and 110% willing to volunteer, despite the alarmingly high risk of failure.
Suggestion: Dick Grayson

Fortress of Solitude

The Phantom Zone Projector is hidden in the Fortress of Solitude. This is Superman's remote Arctic getaway, where he goes to be alone. Batman really needs the Projector, so he faces a long flight in the Batwing with Robin to get there.

Debut Robin

It's Dick's first mission with Batman, and he has a new name: Robin. He's promised to follow orders – even if those orders are to squeeze inside the dangerous atomic cauldron the Projector is stored in.

Batwing is poorly camouflaged in the icy Arctic landscape

Did you know?

The Fortress of Solitude is guarded by Kryptonian Robot Guards, from Superman's home planet.

Justice League

Batman works with Superman in a team of Super Heroes called the Justice League but he does not fit in very well. Batman always wants to be out in front. It makes other heroes such as Superman and Wonder Woman feel sidelined.

The Fortress of Solitude is huge. Finding the front door will be hard.

Batman races ahead – unused to waiting for a partner

Phantom Zone Projector

The Phantom Zone Projector is a device that can send villains to a prison in another dimension! Superman uses it to send his foes away, giving Batman the brilliant idea to use it on the Joker.

Harley Quinn

The Joker's girl buddy

ANYTHING FOR YOU, SUGAR PLUM!

Bodice with contrasting black-and-red pattern

Harley Quinn is the Joker's most trusted partner-in-crime. She knows he's bad to the bone, but she'll do anything for him. Harley is very loyal to the Joker and often helps him think of his most extreme plans.

Party dress

Like a jester, Harley wears a dual-coloured costume – black on one side and red on the other. She carries a huge mallet to squash anyone who gets in her way.

Roller skates help her make a speedy getaway from her crimes

Life in the fast lane

Harley is a daredevil who is not afraid of anything! This makes her the perfect partner for the Joker's criminal, and often dangerous, plans. She grabs on to the Joker's ride and races toward trouble.

Did you know?

Harley has lots of nicknames for the Joker, including "Mr J." and "sugar plum". He calls Harley his "girl buddy".

Blonde hair pulled back into a conventional style

Doctor's notes on her favourite patient – the Joker!

Glasses are a more subtle accessory than a face mask

Hint of Harley's favourite checked pattern

Hard-to-spot Harley disguises

Everyday citizen
Harley can tone down her quirky style and look just like everyone else when she needs to blend in.

Dr Harleen Quinzel
Harley uses her doctor identity to look more trustworthy. No one would suspect a distinguished doctor of being a Rogue!

Doctor, doctor!

Before she teamed up with the Joker, Harley was a respected doctor named Harleen Quinzel. She met the Joker while he was her patient at Arkham Asylum. She was meant to stop his criminal ways, but instead she joined his life of crime.

The Joker's plan

The Joker has tried to take over the Gotham City Energy Facility. He has tried to cause trouble at Jim Gordon's retirement gala. Still, Batman won't take him seriously! The Joker does not give up easily. His latest plan will finally prove that he is Batman's number one foe!

All part of the plan...

Batman uses the Phantom Zone Projector to blast the Joker into a prison in a totally different dimension. The Joker is still smiling though, and it isn't just because Batman is paying him attention. He has a plan!

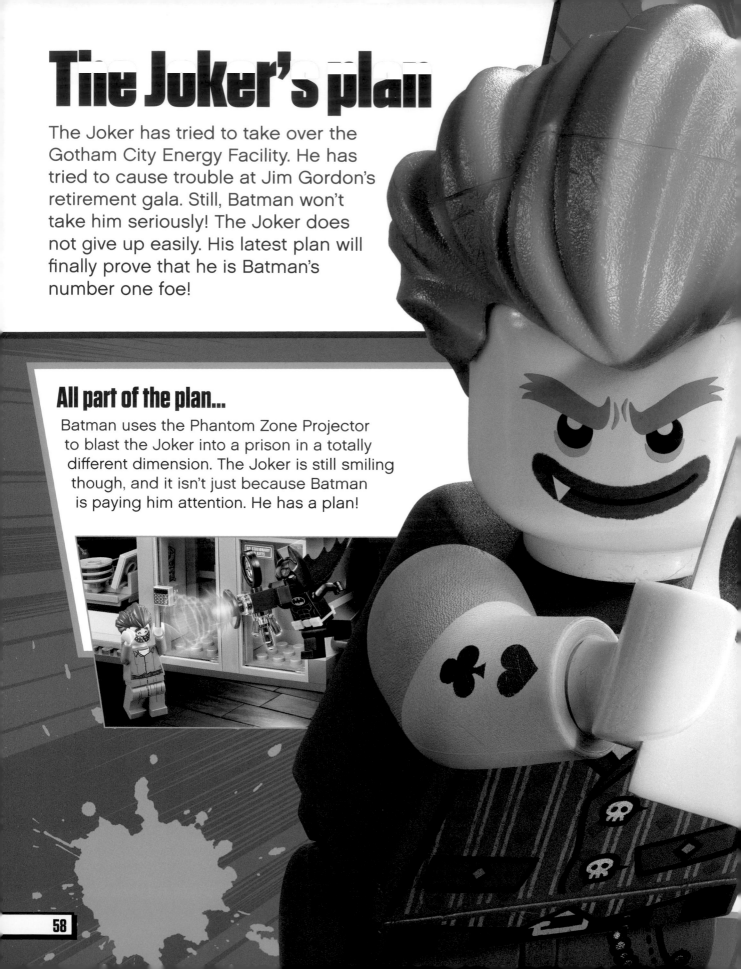

1. Get back to Gotham City

The Joker does not plan to stay in the Phantom Zone for long. He is plotting to return to Gotham City and take over the city once and for all. Everyone will have to follow his rules from now on!

2. Make some home improvements

The Joker thinks that Wayne Manor will make the perfect base for his new leadership. He plans to replace the tasteful decor with brightly coloured, joke-themed items on his return.

3. Prove Batman wrong

The Joker hopes his takeover of Gotham City will show Batman that they really are worst enemies. Finally, Batman might take their relationship seriously!

Family and friends

When the Joker set off his most extreme scheme ever, Batman needs help more than ever before! It has taken some time but Batman finally realises that people can be as helpful as the gadgets he has relied upon in the past. He makes room on the walls of Wayne Manor for some new portraits of his friends and family.

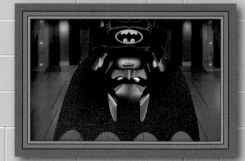

The gang!

Caught on camera

Batman still likes taking selfies, but he has also started taking pictures of his friends and fellow heroes. They deserve a record of their awesome adventures, too!

Robin

Dreams come true

Dick has everything he ever dreamed of: a new home, a new family and a glittery new cape! Batman even thinks he is a worthy Super Hero – what can be better than that?

Batgirl

Working together

Barbara Gordon is now a crime-fighter by day *and* by night. She has adapted quickly to being a masked Super Hero, fighting villains alongside Batman and his other allies.

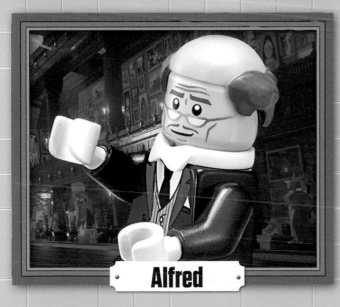

Alfred

Happy helper

As always, Alfred is happy to help when Batman needs him. He is even happier that Batman has opened his heart and home to new friends and family, just as Alfred had hoped.

Which Gotham City good guy are you?

Members of a team need to work together, but they don't all have to think or act the same. Which one of Gotham City's heroes are you most like? Take this quiz to find out!

Answer each of the following questions by picking one answer. Write down the letter of each answer you choose.

1. What do you think is your best quality?

A I am decisive. I always know just what to do to save the day.

B I'm a fast learner! I'm nimble and quick, too.

C I am a good source of wisdom. I am also happy to perform menial tasks, if required.

D I love to be part of team. I rally everyone to work together.

2. A villain has captured one of your friends. How do you persuade the villain to let them go?

A Easy. I'd single-handedly karate-chop them in front of an adoring crowd.

B I'd somersault in front of them and then dazzle them with my glitter cape.

C Perhaps I'd distract them with a cup of tea and a plate of French fancies.

D I'd get out my megaphone and call all my other teammates to help.

3. You're asked out to dine with the mayor of Gotham City. What do you choose from the menu?

A Lobster thermidor, of course.

B Me? Dining with the mayor? Hot diggity-dog! Ermm… a hot dog, maybe?

C I don't think that's appropriate. Surely I should be serving the mayor's meal?

D Just coffee and doughnuts – nothing too fancy.

4. Are you comfortable with expressing your emotions?

A I don't talk about feelings. I don't have any. I've never seen one.

B Yeah! Why wouldn't I be? Everything's so AWESOME!

C Indeed. But I try to do it in the most discreet way possible.

D Honest and open are my middle names.

5. Superman is having a party at the Fortress of Solitude and he invites everyone except you. What is your reaction?

A He did what?! I mean… I didn't want to go anyway. He's so lame.

B That would have been cool, but we can have our own awesome party in the Batcave!

C No offence taken. I am sure Superman has his own butler.

D Not an issue. I'm needed here in Gotham City 24/7 anyway.

Check your answers!

Mostly As:
You are Batman. You are a born leader, but try to remember that working with others can make your life easier, too.

Mostly Bs:
You are most like Dick. You are super enthusiastic, you are loyal and you flat out refuse to let anything get you down.

Mostly Cs:
Like Alfred, you are happy staying out of the limelight. Your team knows they just couldn't get by without you though.

Mostly Ds:
You are most like Barbara. You are a real team player, and people trust you because you say exactly what you think.

Editor Beth Davies
Senior Designer Lauren Adams
Pre-Production Producer Rebecca Fallowfield
Producer Louise Daly
Managing Editor Paula Regan
Design Managers Guy Harvey and Jo Connor
Art Director Lisa Lanzarini
Publisher Julie Ferris
Publishing Director Simon Beecroft

Batman created by Bob Kane with Bill Finger

DK would like to thank Randi Sørensen, Paul Hansford,
Martin Leighton Lindhardt at the LEGO Group; Ben Harper at
Warner Bros.; and Hannah Dolan, Nathan Martin, and Sam
Bartlett at DK for editorial and design assistance.

First published in Great Britain in 2017
by Dorling Kindersley Limited
80 Strand, London WC2R 0RL
A Penguin Random House Company

10 9 8 7 6 5 4 3 2 1
001–297915–Jan/2017

Page design Copyright ©2017 Dorling Kindersley Limited

A WORLD OF IDEAS:
SEE ALL THERE IS TO KNOW

www.LEGO.com
www.dk.com